Glasgow Art Deco

RICHARD DREW PUBLISHING
Glasgow

First published 1985 by
Richard Drew Publishing Ltd
6 Clairmont Gardens
Glasgow G3 7LW

British Library Cataloguing in Publication Data

Kenna, Rudolph
  Glasgow Art Deco.
  1. Architecture——Scotland——Glasgow
  (Strathclyde)   2. Art Deco——Scotland——
  Glasgow (Strathclyde)
  I. Title
  720'.9414'43   NA981.G5/

  ISBN 0 86267 093 4

Typeset by Morton Word Processing Ltd, Scarborough
Printed in Great Britain by Butler & Tanner Ltd, Frome and London

Acknowledgments

I am extremely grateful to Richard Dell of Strathclyde Regional Archives for permission to select and reproduce material from the Archives' extensive collection of negatives – photographic records of properties for use in Glasgow's valuation court, dating from the period 1920–1940. I am also indebted to his courteous and efficient staff. Antony Kamm read the first draft of the typescript and I am most grateful for his well-considered and constructive criticism.

Contents

Introduction

Glasgow is now widely recognised as the Victorian City *par excellence*, a veritable treasure-house of nineteenth and early twentieth-century architecture and ornament, but by the beginning of the interwar period the epoch of grandiose public, commercial and domestic developments was over; money was scarce and for architects and craftsmen alike the prospects were bleak.

Notwithstanding the economic doldrums of the Thirties, several notable buildings were erected in typical Art Deco style, two of the best-known being Montague Burton's premises at the corner of Argyle Street and Buchanan Street (designed by a Leeds architect, Harry Wilson) and James Templeton and Company's colourful factory extension facing Glasgow Green (George Boswell, 1936), but Glasgow Art Deco mainly consisted of cafés, pubs, restaurants and shops – consumer Art Deco which did much to brighten up the Depression-stricken city. Ironically, these were the very places that were most susceptible to change: in the twenty-year period 1955–1975 the vast majority vanished; some were stylistically updated (usually in execrable taste), many more were buried amid the rubble of urban redevelopment. Happily some of the establishments which feature in the accompanying illustrations have survived for the time being; one can, for example, still lunch in the Rogano (handsomely restored in 1984), enjoy a pint of Guinness in the Thornwood Bar or the Tavern, or sip a restorative coffee in the Central Café. Art Deco pubs have fared marginally better than Art Deco cafés and restaurants, and one long-established west end restaurant – Hubbard's – now enjoys a new lease of life as a trendy pub.

The early Art Deco style originated in the avant-garde decorative idioms of the years immediately preceding the First World War, in particular the fashionable decoration inspired by the exotic and colourful décor which Leon Bakst produced for Diaghilev's Ballet Russe. It was seen at its most sumptuous at the Paris *Exposition des Arts Decoratifs* of 1925 – the show which gave Art Deco its name. Towards the end of the decade the stylised human and animal forms, floral motifs and curvilinear shapes characteristic of mid-Twenties' Art Deco were largely superseded by quasi-Egyptian motifs and hard angular shapes, derived from Cubist and Abstract paintings and the chevrons and zigzag patterns of the American skyscraper style (itself deeply influenced by pre-Columbian art).* At this time there was also a significant change in the preferred materials: designers of the Twenties had explored the luxurious qualities of handworked materials and finishes such as exotic woods, ivory, marquetry and lacquer; the Thirties, on the other hand, saw the increasing use of stainless steel, aluminium, chromed metal, glass and faïence, a trend indicative of the growing commitment to a future of machine-production. The resulting shops, cinemas and department stores differed from the experimental productions of the Continental school in being ambivalently Moderne rather than ruthlessly Modernist: their 'cosmetic' facades and trimmings put them far beyond the Functionalist pale.

Thirties Moderne was, in effect, a 'middle-of-the-road' alternative to the coldly intellectual aesthetic of unadorned glass, steel and concrete, a late flowering of that deeply-rooted decorative impulse which was shortly to be virtually eliminated through the exigencies of the Second World War, post-war austerity and the remorseless march of the International Style.

While the average man and woman of the middle-to-late-Thirties would assuredly have possessed some Art Deco/Moderne artifacts and ornaments (we may take it for granted that gaudily coloured plaster statuettes bordering on kitsch were more in evidence than Lalique moulded glass vases or Chiparus chryselephantine dancers), they would have remained on mere nodding terms with the fabled 'spirit of the age' had it not been for places of refreshment, relaxation and entertainment. Only the rich or near-rich could afford to avail themselves of the services of Oliver Hill, John Duncan Miller, Denham Maclaren and other fashionable architects and decorators, but people of moderate means could at least have a snack in a newly refurbished tea-room (bright with coloured tube lighting and glittering with faïence and faceted mirrors) then proceed to the cinema to watch Hollywood musicals and similar films where the sets were full of Deco touches.

Much popular Thirties' design was, as it were, a natural reaction to the decorative 'overkill' of the Victorians and Edwardians. 'The idea of hiding the useful or structural, or dressing it up to look like something else, is forever discredited, swept away with the same vigour that all forms of hypocrisy were swept away by the war and post-war generations.' Or so *The Studio Year Book of Decorative Art* thought in 1933. In reality the cult of the new, which was to grow to monstrous proportions and entail horrendous sacrifices thirty or forty years on, was at that time still only in its infancy, and principally manifested itself in a preference for glossy-surfaced materials. Now the wheel has turned full circle: the post-Modernist phenomenon of Ornamentalism – the widespread revival of interest in the decorative arts and crafts – can be seen as a reaction against the Bauhaus Modern style which swept everything before it in the aftermath of the Second World War and all but banished ornament and decoration from the land. Interestingly enough, there is a strong Art Deco/Moderne influence at work in Ornamentalism, particularly evident in the creation of anti-functional furniture and accessories and in explorations of the decorative potential of coloured neon and reflective materials such as faïence, mirrored glass and shiny metals.

The 1938 Glasgow Exhibition, held in Bellahouston Park, epitomised the romantic side of Thirties Moderne and also reflected the somewhat woolly, 'pie in the sky' social idealism of the late-Thirties: Thomas Tait's strikingly futuristic Tower of Empire (beacon lights from the observation galleries could be seen a hundred miles away) soared triumphantly above a dazzling array of white and colour rendered pavilions, a reassuringly rose-coloured vision of technological developments to come. Thankfully, none of the 13,500,000 people who braved the atrocious and unseasonable weather to visit the Exhibition had their spirits further dampened by a preview of the dreary peripheral housing schemes, jerry-built high-rise flats and faceless office blocks that were to be the main architectural innovations of the next several decades.

Suggestions for Further Reading

Arwas, Victor.   Art Deco (1980)

Atwell, David.   Cathedrals of the Movies (1980)

Battersby, Martin.   The Decorative Twenties (1969)
The Decorative Thirties (1971)

Dean, David.   The Thirties: Recalling the English Architectural Scene (1983)

Garland, Madge.   The Indecisive Decade: The World of Fashion and Entertainment in the Thirties (1968).

Sharp, Dennis.   The Picture Palace (1969).

*It is worthy of remark that in his later decorative work – in particular his interiors at 78 Derngate, Northampton (1916) and his earlier Cloister Room at Miss Cranston's Ingram Street tea-room (1911) – Glasgow's own Charles Rennie Mackintosh anticipated the geometrical idiom of the late-Twenties and early-Thirties.

The typical Glasgow pub of the period 1890–1930 consisted of a large public bar, high ceilinged and dominated by a huge island counter, in the centre of which stood a gantry supporting a row of whisky barrels. Not until the Thirties was its position seriously challenged. The new type of pub had little of the panache of its late-Victorian or Edwardian predecessor: the dream palace – that is to say the cinema – had superseded the liquor palace to become the principal avenue of mass escapism. Drinking habits, too, were changing; whisky was being consumed in smaller quantities, and bottled proprietary blends were now more popular than publicans' 'special blends', with the result that the gantry with its barrels was fast becoming an anachronism. And while older bar-patrons still went in for perpendicular drinking, members of the younger generation were certainly not averse to a little comfort. Many Thirties' pubs were reconstructions of existing licensed premises: false hanging ceilings were installed (lofty interiors were most definitely passé), slender cast-iron pillars with foliated capitals were encased in laminated wood, and massive bar fitments were removed, allowing for a greater provision of seats and tables than had hitherto been possible. In the smaller sort of pub, shelving of polished armour-plate glass took the place of the traditional carved wooden bar-back.

Cocktail and lounge bars were a development of the interwar period and were fairly numerous in the Glasgow of the Thirties (though it is interesting to note that cocktails were dispensed in so-called American bars such as MacSorley's at the turn of the century). The décor of the cocktail bar was intended to reflect its up-to-date and would-be-sophisticated image, hence the extensive use of decoratively grained wood veneers, tinted mirrors (often engraved with perky Moderne motifs such as stylised cocktail shakers, glasses and bottles), tubular lighting, chromium-plated bar furniture and geometric-patterned curtains. Bar counters, of course, were suitably streamlined: round or oval island bars were relieved with strips of chrome or anodised aluminium or decorative bands of contrasting veneers, while long bars were given rounded ends. In Moderne-style pubs of the late-Thirties the ceiling above the counter was frequently lowered to form a canopy which was often fitted

with concealed lighting. Counter fronts were occasionally faced with moulded glass bricks, tiles, Vitrolite or coloured mirror. Vitrolite (an opaque sheet-glass with a smooth surface and a back ridged to facilitate bedding in mastic) was available in a wide range of colours and could be sandblasted and painted. Some large buildings, such as factories and cinemas, were entirely faced with the material, and shop, café and pub fronts in multicoloured Vitrolite were ubiquitous in the late-Thirties. Curved bar fronts and structural columns were frequently covered in Vitroflex (small facets of mirrored or opaque glass in various colours, mounted on fabric), which could be bent in a concave or convex direction and etched with decorative designs. Vitrolite and Vitroflex were manufactured by Pilkington Bros. Ltd. Bakelite, extensively used in the Thirties for radio cabinets and telephone receivers, was also employed in laminated sheet form as a covering for bar tops and tables and as a facing for counter fronts; it was unaffected by moisture or alcohol and was impervious to hot liquids. Bakelite decorative veneers, applied to plywood, were sometimes used to surface interior walls and flush doors. A bewildering variety of wood veneers were available, and among solid woods, teak was highly popular. In many refurbished English pubs of the Thirties, old-fashioned wooden bar-pulls struck the only discordant note; Scottish pubs of the same period usually had chromium-plated counter founts, and by 1940 the long-established firm of Gaskell and Chambers Ltd. were advertising their new oval pattern Catalin Founts in coloured plastic.

Low-relief panels were a popular form of decoration for Thirties' pub interiors; a decorative cliché of the period was a panel which depicted a chic female figure with a greyhound straining at the leash, both highly stylised (in the Twenties and Thirties, greyhounds, impeccably streamlined, were a popular fashion accessory).

Since Victorian times, decorative glass – acid embossed, brilliant-cut and sandblasted – had been one of the principal ingredients of pub design, and it continued to be so in the interwar period. Thirties' pub interiors were frequently decorated with large sheets of mirrored glass in shades of gold, peach (by far the most popular), red, blue, grey and green, while pub windows were stained, sandblasted, or brilliant-cut in a wide range of Moderne themes and patterns. The technique of shaded sandblasting was increasingly employed to achieve fine gradations of tone.

Imaginative artificial lighting was a feature of many Thirties' pubs, cafés and restaurants, a development heralded by the foyer of the Strand Palace Hotel (1930) with its illuminated glass balustrades. In some pubs, the lighting was diffused by means of reflectors or luminous tubes concealed in cornices or troughs, in others the lighting fixtures were wall appliqués (frequently in triangular shapes of tinted glass) or decorative pendants composed of laminated coloured glass panels. Mirrored bar-backs were often highlighted by means of coloured tubular lighting. Some brilliantly creative 'futuristic' lighting fittings were produced by specialist firms such as Troughton and Young Ltd., Helophane Ltd., and the Merchant Adventurers Ltd.

In the Thirties, Scottish publicans, many of whom still spread sawdust on the floors of their premises to absorb spillage, had not yet reconciled themselves to the prospect of wall-to-wall carpets. Rubber flooring was, however, a hardwearing and attractive alternative to the traditional linoleum and was available in a large selection of colours and inlaid Moderne designs.

*   *   *   *

Cafés, mainly owned by first generation Italian immigrants, spread throughout Scotland in the wake of the Temperance Movement, which reached its peak of influence shortly before the First World War. At the height of Temperance agitation, it seemed not unlikely that the café would one day supersede the pub in the affections of thirsty Scots. Somewhat perturbed by this alarming prospect, licensed trade spokesmen fought back, maliciously retailing stories concerning 'alien' café proprietors who surreptitiously supplied whisky in place of non-alcoholic beverages – just the sort of underhand ploy that foreigners might be expected to indulge in.

Cafés were a particularly useful amenity in a city like Glasgow, where flat-dwelling on the Continental model was customary and where many families lived in overcrowded, claustrophobic conditions. Glasgow cafés were in fact an integral part of the tenement way of life, and although they frequently rejoiced in high-falutin names such as 'Café del Rio' and 'Café de Luxe', they were almost invariably unpretentious places: the typical café consisted of a front shop and a back sitting-room where customers could linger over soft drinks or specialities such as the ever-popular 'McCallum' (vanilla ice-cream with raspberry juice). The usual seating arrangement took the form of one or more rows of high-backed booths, which provided a welcome modicum of privacy. Cafés – which throughout the Twenties and Thirties continued to be owned and operated by families of Italian extraction – were perhaps the most characteristic expression of Glasgow Art Deco, with boldly lettered fascias and shiny colourful frontages, carried out in Vitrolite, marble, terrazzo, wood and metal.

1

Licensed premises of Patrick
Griffin, 65–67 London Street (now
London Road), photographed in
September 1926 shortly after
completion; the architect was
A. Hamilton Scott. An unusual pub
in a transitional style, somewhere
between Edwardian Classical and
Thirties Moderne, it was equipped
with an octagonal island bar
counter.

2

The Mermaid, 159 James Street, March 1929. In these days of rapidly ascending prices it is worthy of note that McEwan's 90s ale and other strong draught beers remained 6d per pint right up until the outbreak of the Second World War.

3

The same premises after alterations by A. Hamilton Scott, March 1930. A small east end pub with geometric influence evident in the treatment of the external woodwork.

Two well-known city centre bars, photographed in April 1930 – both have windows etched with angular decorative motifs characteristic of the 'jazz age':

4

The Garrick Tavern, 78 Wellington Street. Situated directly opposite the Alhambra Theatre; its walls were decorated with show business memorabilia. George Owen, the Garrick's proprietor, also ran several other 'theatreland' pubs, including the Bay Horse in West Nile Street, remodelled in Deco fashion in 1934 and still in existence, though much changed.

5

The Grant Arms, 188–190 Argyle Street. In 1937 the first-floor warehouse became part of the pub, being reconstructed to form a Moderne-style lounge bar. John Grant's other catering enterprises included the Grand Central Hotel, Belfast, and the Buchanan Arms Hotel, Drymen.

6

The Tavern, 194 Tollcross Road, February 1931. Formerly a ruinous tenement property, it was revamped in 1930 in 'Tudorbethan' fashion with cement finish and oak strips in imitation of half-timbered construction; the architect was John A. Reid. Still-extant pub which retains much of the original interior decoration.

In the Twenties and early-Thirties, Glasgow pubs closed at the shockingly early hour of nine, a hangover from the wartime 'DORA' (Defence of the Realm Act) restrictions. Although ten o'clock closing was instituted in 1932, Captain Percy Sillitoe, the Chief Constable, insisted upon customers leaving licensed premises immediately on closing time.

The Kirk House, 1365 Shettleston Road before and after reconstruction. In 1937, architect Samuel Bunton remodelled and enlarged the premises, creating a spacious pub with laylights and a false hanging ceiling, a 'streamlined Moderne' oval island counter, sitting rooms and a 'family department' for the carry-out trade; the exterior was finished in rustic brick and faïence. The photograph of the new Kirk House was taken in February 1939.

9

The General Wolfe, 789
Gallowgate, July 1938. Designed
by Samuel Bunton in 1937; a small
pub consisting of a public bar, with
sitting room and family dept. The
exterior was clad in cement finished
corrugated asbestos sheets and
ceramic tiles.

Lettering, often very large in scale and heavily stylised, was the dominant feature of many Thirties' pub fronts:

=== **10** ===

The Moy, 232 Paisley Road, (February 1937).

=== **11** ===

The Neuk, 243–245 Dumbarton Road (June 1938). Designed by Samuel Bunton, this was such a popular pub before the war that on specially busy nights, such as Fridays and Saturdays, a commissionaire had to be employed to stand at the door and ensure that the premises did not become overcrowded. The frontage was clad in black Vitrolite with a base of glass bricks, illuminated from behind by means of coloured lights which produced a diffused effect. Inside, the counter was also faced with glass bricks, again with coloured back-lighting.

12

The Regal, 1377–79 Argyle Street, July 1937. A standard Vitrolite-faced Glasgow pub of the Thirties; note the etched glass with stylised thistle motif.

13

Licensed premises of Samuel Dow Ltd., 226 Great Western Road, photographed in July 1936 shortly after completion; the architects were Messrs. Lennox and MacMath. A popular west end pub, still in existence under another name, it originally consisted of a public bar, with a large sitting room at the rear of the premises, but in 1938–39 James W. Weddell added a lounge and a cocktail bar; the latter was located in the basement and was decorated with stylised designs intended to represent cocktails such as White Lady, Manhattan and Angel's Kiss; the pub's teak frontage was also extended at that time. Traditional Scottish pubs were male preserves, but the new lounge and cocktail bars of the late-Thirties freely admitted women *when escorted by male companions.*

The Punch Bowl, 1512 Maryhill Road in August 1937 and again in March 1939. An Edwardian pub with sub Art Nouveau detail, remodelled in an attractive Moderne style.

The Gartocher Bar, 1618–1622
Shettleston Road, August 1938. A
small bothy-type pub, reconstructed
and enlarged in 1937 by architect
William Ross to form a spacious
public bar with an island counter,
sitting rooms and 'family
department'; the exterior was faced
with rustic bricks and faïence.

The Bay Horse, 964 Pollokshaws Road, March 1937. A south-side pub with characteristic Moderne styling. Instead of being glazed, in typical pub fashion, with etched glass, the windows are used for display purposes, a hallmark of the new 'sophisticated' cocktail and lounge bars of the late-Thirties.

Variety Bar, 15 Cowcaddens Street, April 1938. A delightfully light-hearted pub exterior with decorative motifs which allude to the near-proximity of theatres and music halls.

It is a popular misconception that Glasgow pubs of the interwar period were invariably grim utilitarian 'spit and sawdust' establishments; on the contrary, many boasted an enviable standard of comfort and service, with immaculate furnishings and fittings and attentive bar staff, smartly attired in uniform jackets, white shirts and bow ties.

Licensed premises of St Mungo Vintners Ltd., 314 Clyde Street, January 1939 (A. McEwan and Co. Ltd., shopfitters). A particularly handsome Moderne bar, still in existence but sadly altered.

As late as April 1939, Glasgow's puritanical licensing magistrates prohibited all pub games, including darts, draughts and dominoes; they subsequently raised the ban on draughts and dominoes but reaffirmed their opposition to darts!

The Thornwood, 722–724
Dumbarton Road, as it appeared in
February 1939. This was the last
oasis before the notorious 'dry' area
of Whiteinch, where a majority of
the local residents had exercised
their democratic rights under the
Temperance (Scotland) Act of 1913
and had voted in 1924 to keep the
district free of the nefarious 'drink
traffic'. It survives in remarkably
good condition and has a Vitrolite
exterior in primrose and black with
a neon-illuminated fascia. The
interior, untouched by the
'improver', is delightfully evocative
of its period, with dark walnut
veneered panelling and ceiling
laylights. The architect was James
Taylor and the shopfitter James
Rodger.

═ 21 ═

The Nipp, 416–418 Parliamentary Road, photographed in August 1939. Moderne-style pub in a once-populous district of Glasgow, since devastated by the city planners. The Nipp had a semi-circular bar counter with an overhead canopy containing luminous tubes; the architect was James Taylor Thomson.

The 1939 war budget increased the duty on beer and spirits; beer went up to 7d per pint while whisky, formerly 'twelve an' a tanner a bottle', varied in price from 14/3 to 15/- per five gill bottle.

Pub exterior at 64–66 Broomielaw, April 1940. Typical Moderne treatment, with pronounced horizontal emphasis and Vitrolite facing.

In the autumn of 1940, the shortage of male bar staff forced Glasgow's licensing magistrates to remove a ban on barmaids, which they had imposed many years previously; the bailies, however, cautiously insisted that barmaids employed in the city's pubs should be at least twenty-five years old!

23

Café D'Oré, 101–105 Dundas Street, July 1932. Designed in 1930 by Messrs. Gaff, Gillespie and Kidd, and subsequently enlarged.

24

The Derby, 60 Argyle Street, August 1932. Designed by a Motherwell architect, A. Victor Wilson; the fluid Moderne lettering and styling, so different from the angular motifs current at this time, were to become increasingly characteristic of Glasgow cafés in the Thirties.

25

Dé Simone's, 53 Hyndland Street, July 1935. West end café with geometric 'jazz modern' detail. Prior to the Sixties' decade with its burgeoning youth culture, permissiveness and affluence, a 'night out' for young people of opposite sexes frequently meant a visit to the local café and a prolonged tête-à-tête over raspberry ices or plates of peas and vinegar!

The incorporation of leaded glass in the frontages of Glasgow cafés was a practice which began in the Edwardian period and continued throughout the Twenties and into the early-Thirties, to be superseded by an integrated Moderne lettering and fascia treatment:

26

The Wheatsheaf, 8 Cornwall Street, April 1929: typical of Twenties' café styling before the decorative innovations of the following decade; notice the sitting room, fitted into the first floor of the tenement.

27

New Bridge Café, 38 Bridge Street, June 1931.

28

Café de Luxe, 1102 Dumbarton Road, March 1932.

29

The Strand, 168 Dumbarton Road, February 1933.

30

Lido Café, 219 Saracen Street,
photographed in September 1937.
Small café in working-class district
of north Glasgow, designed by
James Wilson (shopfitter) in 1936.

The Glasgow café in its tenement milieu:

━━━ **31** ━━━

The Parade Bungalow,
506 Alexandra Parade,
September 1931.

━━━ **32** ━━━

Demarco Bros., 322–330 Garscube Road,
August 1936.

━━━ **33** ━━━

Café D'Oré, 14 Killermont Street,
August 1936.

━━━ **34** ━━━

The Cumbrae, 4 Killermont Street,
June 1938.

━━━ **35** ━━━

Black Cat, 1223–25 Govan Road,
May 1939.

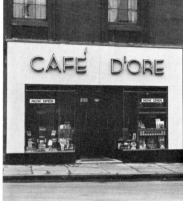

36

The Rio Grande Café, 21 Bridge Street, undergoing alterations in May 1939.

37

Refurbished as the Café del Rio (photographed in August 1939). This café survives, although the upper storeys of the tenement have been demolished.

A number of Glasgow cafés took their names from neighbouring cinemas:

═══ **38** ═══

Broadway, 1198 Shettleston Road, August 1939.

═══ **39** ═══

Lyceum, 853 Govan Road, August 1939.

A selection of Glasgow café lettering and fascia styles; these were invariably colourful and decorative, the essence of Thirties' popular Moderne.

=== **40** ===

St Enoch Café, 46–48 Howard Street,
July 1931.

=== **41** ===

The Nauld, 664 Cumbernauld Road,
February 1933.

=== **42** ===

Victoria Café, 349 Victoria Road, August 1935; below the fascia, that recurrent Thirties' motif, the radiating sun; it appeared on all sorts of objects, from the radiators of Albion motor lorries to the deep-frying apparatus in fish and chip shops.

43

Criterion, 273 Rutherglen Road,
March 1936.

44

Coia's, 1403 Shettleston Road,
August 1937.

45

The Favourite, 930 Maryhill Road,
August 1939.

46

Café Moderne, 1012 Pollokshaws Road, April 1940; a particularly good example of back-lit, three-dimensional fascia lettering.

47

Central Café, 27 Saltmarket, photographed in August 1939. One of the few city centre cafés which still retain their colourful Vitrolite fronts and distinctively lettered fascias.

Restaurants, Snack Bars & Tea-rooms

Fast service restaurants, snack bars and milk bars came into vogue in the Thirties and were specially prevalent in the near vicinity of railway stations. Their characteristic features were long counters – Vitrolite or Bakelite faced or wood veneered, and frequently adorned with Moderne motifs such as the ubiquitous sunburst – and rows of gleaming chromed metal stools. The walls were sometimes decorated with tinted mirrors, silvered or coloured opaque Vitroflex, or painted murals. The Thirties decade was also the Indian summer of the elegant and economical tea-room/restaurant; in London Oliver Bernard created the interiors of the famous Lyons' Corner Houses – the very essence of popular Art Deco – while in Glasgow, restaurateurs James Craig Ltd., R.A. Peacock and Son, Ltd., and Walter Hubbard Ltd., provided similar facilities for partakers of that traditional Scottish repast, high tea. Now alas, the stylish tea-rooms and restaurants of the interwar years have been superseded by utilitarian takeaways whose by-product is mountains of litter. Some of the best-known Glasgow restaurants of the Thirties were strictly teetotal, a tradition which dated back to the famous Cranston tea-rooms of the early 1900s; it was not until 1936 that the huge Ca'doro Restaurant in Union Street was granted a public house licence.

Of the licensed restaurants of the same period, the Rogano in Exchange Place is a rare and precious survivor. The long-established Rogano bodega bar was acquired in April 1935 by John Grant of the Royal Restaurant, West Nile Street and the Grant Arms, Argyle Street; at his behest the premises underwent major alterations. The Rogano oyster bar, which opened on Wednesday, 23rd October 1935, was modelled on the celebrated Prunier fish restaurants in Paris and London; on the menu were numerous sea food dishes, including bouillabaisse, and the appointments of the kitchen included tanks containing live eels and rainbow trout. The dining room, known as the Lucullus Room, was decorated with murals depicting mermaids and other mythical denizens of the deep. The alterations were carried out by Messrs. A. McEwan and Co., Ltd.

Georgic Restaurant, 28–40 Union Street, photographed in March 1931. Designed in 1929 by Messrs. Whyte and Galloway for R.A. Peacock and Son, Ltd., it consisted of a ground-floor shopping hall, with a tea-room, restaurant and ballroom situated respectively on the upper three floors. Diffused illumination, provided by panelled glass pendants, wall appliqués and continuous cornice lighting, was a feature of the interiors.

Premises of Walter Hubbard Ltd., 510 Great Western Road, June 1931. Designed in 1929 by architect James Lindsay; the frontage is faced with glazed terracotta. A remodelling of a long-established Hillhead baker's shop and restaurant. Latterly part of City Bakeries Ltd., Hubbard's closed down in December 1970; the building has since been reopened as a pub.

50

Dominion Restaurant, 251 Sauchiehall Street, photographed in June 1933, immediately after completion; designed by W.J.B. Wright, it had dining facilities on two storeys. An eye-catching example of early Thirties Moderne styling, with angular neon-lit lettering and glass sandblasted in uninhibited 'jazz modern' fashion.

Shop and tea-room of Messrs. James Campbell and Sons at 20–22 Glassford Street, June 1935 (Archibald Hamilton Ltd., shopfitters).

52

Ramshorn Restaurant, 93 Ingram
Street, September 1936.

53

Milk Bar, Central Station, photographed in August 1936. In the late-Thirties the beverage was extensively promoted by the Milk Marketing Board and milk bars, already well-established in the United States, were opened in many British towns and cities.

54

Typical 'Frying Tonight Deco' as thousands of Glaswegians remember it: Nobile's fish restaurant, 921 Shettleston Road, photographed in March 1936. Judging by the entrance door with its Edwardian or early-Twenties etched glass motif, only the exterior of this set of premises has been remodelled.

Rogano restaurant and sea food bar, 11 Exchange Place, March 1936. In the new premises the Victorian bodega bar was commemorated by a Spanish sherry bar, presided over by Jack, a cocktail expert, formerly on the *Empress of Britain*. Glasgow's finest surviving Art Deco restaurant, the Rogano was restored in 1984 by its present owners, Ind-Coope of Alloa, but the wine shop adjunct, visible in the photograph, no longer exists.

56

Pelican Luncheon Bar,
112 New City Road, March 1937.

=57/58/59=

Berkeley Restaurant, 215 North Street, 227 North Street and 231 North Street, photographed in 1934, 1936 and 1938. All three sets of premises by architect W.J.B. Wright. A long-established and popular Italian restaurant which only recently removed to a new location.

60

Tea-room, 141 Dundas Street, photographed in June 1938 shortly after completion.

61

Helen Howie restaurant,
607 London Road, August 1938.

63

Licensed restaurant, 791 Govan Road, March 1940. Designed the previous year by architect John Robb, the premises consisted of a ground-floor lounge bar and first-floor restaurant.

Cinemas & Dance Halls

In the movie boom years, Glasgow had more cinemas per head of population than any other city outside the United States, and for a time Green's Playhouse, opened in 1925 with 4400 seats, was Europe's largest picture palace. It is, however, to be regretted that no surviving Glasgow cinema can stand comparison with those justly celebrated 'cathedrals of the movies', the Tooting Granada, the Muswell Hill Odeon and the Finsbury Park Astoria. Several of the most remarkable cinemas of the late-Twenties and early-Thirties reflected the Egyptianising trend which arose in part from the tremendous interest in Egyptian art generated by the discovery in 1922 of Tutankhamun's tomb. Quasi-Egyptian Art Deco could be seen elsewhere other than in places of popular entertainment – for example, in the main hall of the Glasgow Eye Infirmary at Sandyford Place (Sir John Burnet, Tait and Lorne, 1935; since greatly altered). Many major cinemas of the Thirties were equipped with cafés, restaurants and soda fountains and also boasted full stage facilities; there were regular appearances by stars of cinema and radio, top bands and vocalists, and daily recitals on mighty Compton or Wurlitzer organs.

The late-Thirties saw the predominance of the super cinemas, most of which were distinguished externally by clean, 'streamlined Moderne' lines and fashionable surfaces such as toughened glass, glazed terracotta and Vitrolite; the cinema, moreover, was no longer a novelty – good acoustics and sightlines were now quite as important as an eye-catching entrance facade. The finest Glasgow cinemas of this date were erected in suburbs such as Anniesland and King's Park, to the designs of Charles J. McNair and James McKissack. Happily still extant, though invariably converted to bingo, they serve to remind us of the vanished era of movie madness, of long queues of film fans and hosts of uniformed flu-nkeys. The Thirties' super cinemas were the largest Art Deco/Moderne buildings to which the general public had ready access, and for their patrons, the illusion of luxury provided by Hollywood Deco would have been heightened by the décor of the cinema auditoriums and foyers. As the premier form of popular entertainment, Thirties' super cinemas really came into their own after dark, when their external features were sharply outlined in neon, proving that the romantic Teutonic concept of the cinema as 'night architecture' was not entirely fanciful.

* * * *

Glaswegians were as fond of ballroom dancing as they were keen on cinema-going. Palais de danse proliferated in the Twenties in response to widespread enthusiasm for fashionable new dances such as the Charleston, the fox-trot, the shimmy and the tango. One of the most popular venues in the city centre was the Locarno, Sauchiehall Street (named, like a number of other ballrooms of its vintage, in honour of that memorable example of interwar *rapprochement*, the Locarno Treaty of 1925). In 1937 there were 202 premises in the city licensed for public dancing; the capacity of these dance halls varied from 56 to 755 but in all they catered for 26,963 dancers. Southsiders frequented the Plaza, Eglinton Toll, or the Cameo at Shawlands, while east-enders flocked to Barrowland or, if they were sufficiently well-heeled, to the new Dennistoun Palais; built in 1937–38 to the design of Charles J. McNair as a replacement for an earlier hall which had been destroyed by fire, the latter had accommodation for 2000 patrons, a tea-room and a soda fountain – but no bar. The exterior was cement rendered and the entrance finished with faïence terracotta.

The Astoria, Round Toll, Possil,
April 1931. Designed by Albert V.
Gardner and opened that same year,
it was the second largest cinema in
Glasgow, with accommodation for
over three thousand people, and
was described at the time of
opening as 'the largest working-
class sound kinema [*sic*] in
Scotland'. The bulky exterior,
finished with rough-cast, was plain
and unadorned with the exception
of the frontage, which was
characteristic of the angular idiom
of the period. External flights of
steps led respectively to the
auditorium and the vestibule, which
was octagonal in shape. The interior
decoration was typical of the 'jazz
modern' stage of Deco, with strong
colours and rising sun motifs. The
auditorium décor was 'carried out
in a modified futuristic fashion', the
design on the ceiling being
'emphasized by four large cubist
lights suspended to form a square
. . . with a huge brightly-coloured
inverted cone slung in the centre'.
In working-class districts children
flocked to the Saturday matinée
where the entertainment was
guaranteed to include lashings of
blood and thunder, and the
managers of some Glasgow cinemas
did not disdain to accept 'jeely jaurs'
(jam jars) in lieu of pennies!

The Mayfair, 33 Sinclair Drive, Battlefield (March 1934). Built to the design of Eric A. Sutherland, it opened on Monday, 1st February 1934 with Madeleine Carroll and Conrad Veidt in *I Was A Spy* – stalls 7d, balcony 1/-. It closed in 1972, and a block of flats now occupies the site.

The Embassy, 146–150
Kilmarnock Road, photographed in
March 1936. Sir Harry Lauder
performed the opening ceremony
on Monday, 3rd February of that
year, when the feature film was
Casino de Paree starring Al Jolson
and Ruby Keeler. Erected by Harry
Winocour and designed by James
McKissack, the faïence-decorated
Embassy was similar in style to the
same architect's Commodore
cinema at Scotstoun; both cinemas
have since been demolished.

67

Kiosk in Westway cinema, Cardonald, photographed in October 1936. The cinema was built in 1934 to the design of Messrs. Bryden, Robertson and Boyd, who also carried out alterations two years later.

68

The State, 1311 Shettleston Road, photographed in August 1937. Erected by George Urie Scott and designed by C.J. McNair, it opened on Monday, 14th June of that year; the opening feature was *Libelled Lady*, with William Powell, Jean Harlow, Myrna Loy and Spencer Tracy. In 1937 Glasgow had 98 cinemas, with a seating capacity of 133,659; this was in addition to twelve theatres and three music halls!

69

The State, 271 Castlemilk Road (King's Park), as it appeared in January 1938. Designed by C.J. McNair for George Urie Scott, it opened the previous December with Ruby Keeler and Lee Dixon in *Ready, Willing and Able*; it had seats for 1600, priced at 6d, 9d and 1/-. The severe 'modernistic' exterior was rendered in roughcast, brick and glazed terracotta.

Striking Moderne styling with an external rendering of faïence: the entrance facade of the Vogue cinema, 265 Langlands Road, Govan (February 1939). It was designed in 1937 by James McKissack who was also responsible for the handsome Vogue in Riddrie, and had seats for 2500 persons; the gala opening took place on Monday, July 4th 1938. The proprietor of the Govan and Riddrie Vogues was George Singleton, whose distinguished Cosmo cinema (1939) in Rose Street is now the Glasgow Film Theatre.

═ 71 ═

Lyceum, 918 Govan Road, February 1939. Designed by C.J. McNair for Caledon Pictures Limited and opened the previous year, it replaced the old Lyceum Theatre – an ex-music hall, later turned into a cinema and destroyed by fire in 1937. Clean uncluttered lines and the use of 'contemporary' materials such as moulded glass bricks, faïence tiling, Vitrolite glass cladding and neon lighting sharply distinguished Thirties' super cinemas like the 2600-seater Lyceum from earlier forms of street architecture such as the traditional ashlar-faced tenements of Glasgow.

═ 72 ═

The Aldwych, 2130 Paisley Road West, June 1939. One of George Singleton's suburban cinemas; a 2500–seater, designed by James McKissack and opened in 1938, it closed in 1963. Cardonald's other cinema, the 1300-capacity Westway (now a bingo hall), was also part of the Singleton Circuit.

The Ascot, Anniesland, February 1940. Designed by Charles J. McNair for Great Western Cinemas Ltd., it was advantageously sited, almost directly opposite Kelvin Court luxury flats; the entrance facade, flanked by two semi-circular towers, was finished in cream, red and black faïence. Lord Provost Patrick Dollan performed the opening ceremony on Wednesday, December 6th 1939 when the feature film was *Shipyard Sally*, a musical comedy starring Gracie Fields (the film's theme song was 'Wish Me Luck As You Wave Me Goodbye'; composed before the outbreak of hostilities, it became the perfect musical accompaniment to mobilisation). The Ascot was solidly constructed to withstand damage by fire and blast, and exits were so plentiful that the audience of 1900 could be out of the building within minutes. In common with many other cinemas of its date it is now used exclusively for bingo and is disfigured by a huge illuminated sign to that effect. A far cry from Cinema's golden years, when thickly carpeted foyers, commissionaires attired like Ruritanian counts, and page-boys in tight-fitting Grand Hotel-style uniforms presaged the escapist delights of Busby Berkeley musicals and Alexander Korda epics.

Entrance to the Cameo ballroom,
42 Kilmarnock Road, September
1939. In anticipation of an
immediate onslaught from the air, a
devastating rain of bombs such as
H.G. Wells had forecast in his film
scenario *Things To Come*, Home
Secretary Sir John Anderson closed
all places of popular entertainment
for two weeks at the start of the
war. On September 14th the
emergency restrictions were
removed, and on the 15th it was
'business as usual' at the city's
cinemas, theatres and dance halls.

Dennistoun Palais de Danse (C.J. McNair), 7 Roselea Drive. The grand opening took place on the night of February 16th 1938. The photograph was taken in September 1938, when 'The Lambeth Walk' was the current dance craze.

Palais de Danse (Fyfe and Fyfe Limited), 201 Dumbarton Road, as it appeared in March 1940; if dancing to the patriotic strains of 'We're Gonna Hang Out The Washing On The Siegfried Line' ceased to amuse, then there were always roller skating sessions! Glasgow experienced its first (daylight) air raid on 19th July 1940; the last raid took place on the night of 23rd March 1943.

77

Barrowland, 236–244 Gallowgate, photographed in March 1940 after the premises had been extended to incorporate an ice-rink. The best-known dance hall in the east end of Glasgow, it was designed in 1933 for Mrs. Margaret McIver by Messrs. Bryden, Robertson and Boyd, who were also responsible for the alterations of 1939–40; the ground floor consisted of a market hall.

Shops & Department Stores

The most stylish British shops of the Thirties were modelled on the avant-garde shops of the late-Twenties in Berlin and other progressive Continental cities. In marked contrast to the flatness of earlier shop exteriors, the new shopfronts were noticeably three-dimensional; improvements in artificial lighting and advances in shop-building techniques (including cantilevered construction and the introduction of windows with frameless angles and non-reflecting glass) facilitated display-in-depth, throwing into prominence subtly illuminated shop and showcase interiors with their tantalising selections of consumer goods. The Thirties' shop frontage was not uncommonly deeply recessed to form a lobby for customers, so that even on wet days window shopping could be a pleasant diversion. Whenever possible shop exteriors were also extended upwards, the additional space being utilised for second-floor display windows or for a large, occasionally over-large, fascia with neon-lit lettering.

The new Art Deco/Moderne shopfronts were sometimes regrettably a law to themselves, showing little or no consideration for neighbouring, earlier shop exteriors, or indeed for the handsome nineteenth-century buildings in which – in Glasgow at any rate – they were usually situated. This was not to be wondered at, in view of the fierce iconoclasm of the interwar years; the word 'Victorian' had become a term of opprobrium: while dismissing Victorian architecture in a few lines of his influential *Shrines and Homes of Scotland* (1938) Sir John Stirling Maxwell was able to assert in all seriousness that 'nearly all the buildings were shoddy and bad'. But notwithstanding its occasional lapse into architectural bad manners vis-à-vis its neighbours, the Thirties' shop exterior could be very attractive in its own right, with surfaces of granite, marble or Portland stone, and chic Moderne lettering and decorative motifs in stainless steel, anodised aluminium or bronze, while the interior was often decorated with figured veneered panelling and mirrored plate glass. Thirties Moderne styling in respect of shop premises was epitomised by comparatively small 'quality' shops such as furriers, jewellers, gentlemen's outfitters, milliners and dressmakers. These, of course, were situated in the more exclusive areas; in working-class districts, where competition was particularly fierce, the lettering was almost invariably the most conspicuous feature of the shop.

78

Quasi-Egyptian detailing on a shopfront at 147 Sauchiehall Street, photographed in January 1928.

= 79 =

Premises of James Grant and Co., house furnishers, 12–16 Jamaica Street, March 1929, as remodelled by Messrs. Gardner and Glen the previous year. The first two storeys of a Victorian warehouse have been remodelled to read as one glass-fronted unit, an elevational treatment typical of commercial Moderne styling; there is a deep display frontage with a central arcade, and the exterior finish is black marble cladding.

Costumiers, 3 Argyle Street, April 1929. Two storeys of a rather plain Victorian building, transformed by Moderne styling, with deep display areas. A good example of first-floor windows used for display; an innovation of the late-Twenties, these were seldom incorporated in new premises after 1935 since it was recognised that they wasted valuable space and diminished natural light; the idea behind them was that the displays would be of particular interest to passengers on the upper decks of trams and buses. Notice the faceted angles to the lower shop windows and the decorative application of zigzags, motifs that were almost as characteristic of late-Twenties' and early-Thirties' Deco as the sunburst.

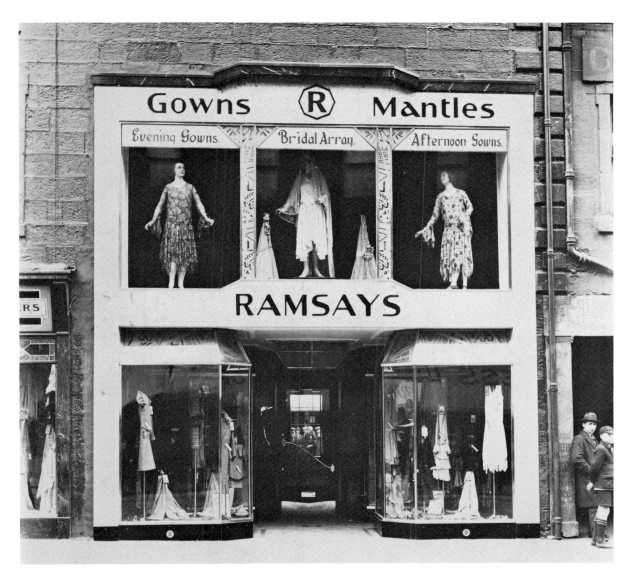

81

Messrs. C. & A. Modes Ltd.,
Sauchiehall and Cambridge Streets,
October 1929. Designed the
previous year by London architects
North, Robin and Wilsdon; a five-
storey building in reinforced
concrete and faïence. The splayed
corners and window strips are
typical of the angular Deco of the
late-Twenties and early-Thirties.

82

Warehouse of Watt Brothers, Ltd., corner of Bath and Hope Streets, photographed in April 1938; built in 1929–30 to the design of Messrs. Keppie and Henderson. The deeply recessed window shopping area at street level contained a number of oblique-angled glass display cases; the cast-iron bays between the stone piers were supplied by Walter MacFarlane and Company.

83

Premises of Marks and Spencer Ltd., 18 Argyle Street, May 1930. The architects were Messrs. James M. Munro and Son.

The Bees shopfront and interior, 320 Pollokshaws Road, April 1933. The gleaming chromed metal chair frames and polished plate glass table tops in this dressmaker's shop were doubtlessly intended to reflect a trendy image; the bentwood chairs – themselves forerunners of the tubular metal chairs of the late-Twenties and early-Thirties – were probably transferred from the earlier Bees establishment in Eglinton Street.

Glasgow Corporation Gas Dept. showrooms, 522 Sauchiehall Street, photographed in March 1935. The arresting frontage was carried out in Hoptonwood stone and black granite, with huge built-up bronze letters, and was lit at night by gas in the form of ornamental lanterns and continuous cornice lighting. Gas wall lanterns, set in fibrous plaster surrounds, were also a feature of the showrooms, which were separated from the service area at the rear by a transverse screen wall with a balcony and ornamental iron grilles – the latter feature, reminiscent of 'atmospheric' interior decoration in the contemporary cinema, was equipped with a projector and screen for demonstration purposes. The architect was A. McInnes Gardner.

87

Moderne-style soft furnishing shop, 373–375 Sauchiehall Street, in process of construction in March 1935. The two-storey frontage survives in an excellent state of preservation; the entrance is deeply recessed on the arcade principle, and the external finish is Roman stone. Built by A. McEwan and Co. Ltd. (shopfitters) to the design of Messrs. E. Pollard and Co. Ltd., London.

88

Martins, Ltd., dyers and cleaners, 310 Sauchiehall Street, September 1935 (A. McEwan and Co. Ltd., shopfitters). A brightly coloured Vitrolite shop front, sandblasted and painted in Moderne fashion.

89

Tailor's premises, 9 Harmony Row, Govan (March 1936). Note the outsize shop fascia, a brash mode of advertising which the proprietors of down-market shops seem to have adopted in response to the unfavourable trading conditions of the Depression years. In working-class districts low prices were the predominant sales factor and were prominently displayed as an incentive to passers-by.

Premises of John Kirsop and Son Ltd., Renfield and West George Streets, photographed in July 1936 (Messrs. John Burnet, Son and Dick, 1935). Here the lofty ground floor of an ornate Victorian office block has been reconstructed to form showrooms and changing rooms on two levels. Portland stone facing, black granite plinth and fittings of bronze, together with discreet Moderne styling and reticent window displays, clearly convey the message that this is a quality men's outfitters (compare with the tailoring establishment in Plate 89). Internally the panelling was mainly of walnut veneer, and fluorescent tube lighting was combined with mirrors to decorative effect.

Cranston's Waverley Hotel, 172 Sauchiehall Street, and the ferro-concrete Marks and Spencer building which replaced it. The latter, designed by James M. Munro and Son, was erected in two stages, in 1935–36 and 1938, when the second of the two photographs was taken; the original M. & S. facade, it will be noticed, was symmetrical.

Moderne influence on Thirties' shop design:

93

Undertaker's premises, 180 Parliamentary Road, August, 1935. It is interesting to note that immortelles in bell jars were still in evidence in the mid-Thirties.

94

Confectioner's shop, incorporated in the Vogue cinema (726 Cumbernauld Road), September 1938.

95

Radio dealer's premises, 532 Cathcart Road, February 1939. The shop formerly belonged to a baker, hence the windmill motif in stained glass.

96

Hairdresser's shop, 117 Saltmarket, June 1937.

97

Premises of Madame Emé Ltd., court dressmaker and furrier, 321–323 Sauchiehall Street, photographed in February 1939. Notice the absence of fascia lettering and window displays; comparatively small semi-luxury shops were among the finest examples of Moderne styling.

Furrier's premises, 54 Buchanan
Street (February 1939). Designed
the previous year by Messrs.
E. Pollard and Co. Ltd. of London;
the frontage was rendered in
faïence.

99

Dress-shop, 77 Union Street, February 1939. Neon-lit, three-dimensional letters, mounted on a neon-outlined obscured glass transom light, form an effective alternative to the conventional lettered fascia panel; the deep entrance, flanked by show windows, is highly typical of Moderne shop design.

Banks & Hotels

Handsome banks had been a feature of the Glasgow scene since early Victorian times, and in the interwar years several noteworthy additions were made to their number. James Miller's Commercial Bank of Scotland (now Royal Bank of Scotland) at the junction of Bothwell and Wellington Streets dates from 1935 and was one of the last commercial buildings in the city to incorporate elements from the Classical vocabulary, a historicist practice which was anathema to the Modernist avant-garde. The giant order of two Corinthian columns *in antis* and the infill of glass and cast-metal panels by Gilbert Bays invoke associations of majestic Graeco-Roman temple fronts with richly ornamented grilles; precisely the sort of thing that led one unkind critic to refer to such buildings as 'temples of Mammon' – yet it can scarcely be denied that they make a more positive contribution to the cityscape than those poker-faced boxes which accommodate every description of public and commercial activity behind curtain-walled exteriors. The Commercial Bank (Royal Bank of Scotland) building at the corner of West George and West Nile Streets, designed by Miller in 1930, has some characteristic Art Deco stonework and ornamental metalwork in one of the geometric 'jazz modern' patterns that were prevalent at that time.

In the larger and more important Glasgow banks of the interwar period the Moderne influence was limited to subsidiary features such as ornamental stonework and metalwork, but several of the smaller banks were more representative of their era. The Commercial Bank of Scotland at 480 Gallowgate (1936) was designed by James McCallum and has one of those corner tower features that were so typical of Thirties Moderne architecture; the main elevations are sheathed in highly polished granite. The Alexandra Park Branch of the Glasgow Savings Bank (1934), designed by Eric A. Sutherland, is surfaced with rustic bricks, with a granite plinth and metal-framed windows. The same architect was also responsible for the Savings Bank's Shettleston Branch (1936).

*   *   *   *

William Beresford Inglis was the architect as well as the proprietor of several well-known Glasgow cinemas, including the Arcadia, Bridgeton and the Toledo, Muirend. His Boulevard Picture House at Knightswood was the first 'atmospheric' cinema in the city. In building a hotel to accommodate visitors to the Glasgow Exhibition of 1938, Inglis, in his own words, decided to 'introduce the lines and colour of the cinema'. The result was the 'streamlined Moderne' and faïence-decorated Beresford Hotel, 460 Sauchiehall Street, designed by James W. Weddell and formally opened on April 28th 1938. There were 198 bedrooms, with one bathroom to every four bedrooms (no major Scottish hotel at that time had a bathroom attached to *every* bedroom); bed and breakfast cost all of twelve shillings and sixpence (62½p). The Beresford Hotel's finest hour was the duration of the Empire Exhibition, the last and most ambitious of the four great Glasgow Exhibitions, but the outbreak of war put paid to its long-term viability, and Inglis was ruined by its failure. Had Thomas Tait's all-metal tower been left standing on Bellahouston Hill,* it would have served as a powerful evocation of the optimistic spirit which, in spite of war clouds, had animated that spectacular event. As it is, the former Beresford Hotel (now Strathclyde University's Baird Hall of Residence) is a flamboyant architectural souvenir of the Exhibition – the Palace of Art building, the only Exhibition structure to remain *in situ*, is dull by comparison.

At the other end of the social spectrum from the Beresford Hotel was the Belgrove Hotel in the Gallowgate (C.J. McNair, 1936), a workingmen's hostel which was erected under the auspices of one Thomas Rodger of Motherwell. The original design was strikingly Moderne and incorporated a conspicuous tower feature in which the vestibule and staircase would have been located, but the plan was subsequently modified, probably on grounds of economy. As built, the accommodation consisted of several floors of cubicles with a lavatory, footbaths and bathroom on each floor. The dining hall, together with billiard and other recreational rooms, was situated on the ground floor. The exterior of the building was finished in cement rendered brick. It speaks volumes for the lack of progress in some areas of social welfare that the Spartan facilities provided by the Belgrove Hotel and similar commercial hostels are still in considerable demand, nearly fifty years later.

*It was removed as a potential navigational guide to bombers.

100

Commercial Bank of Scotland, Bothwell and Wellington Streets, seen here in August 1935; it was designed by James Miller the previous year.

Savings Bank of Glasgow,
Alexandra Park Branch (370–372
Cumbernauld Road), March 1936;
designed in 1934 by Eric A.
Sutherland.

102

Savings Bank of Glasgow,
Shettleston Branch (931
Shettleston Road), August 1937.
Designed the previous year by Eric
A. Sutherland.

81

Commercial Bank of Scotland, Gallowgate Branch (480 Gallowgate), designed in 1936 by James McCallum, Glasgow's Master of Works, and seen here in February 1938. The typical Thirties Moderne clock tower feature makes the most of the corner site while the decorative motif beneath the clock refers to the building's location – opposite the city's meat market.

The Beresford Hotel, 460
Sauchiehall Street, June 1938. Built
of reinforced concrete and faced
with faïence ware in mustard, black
and red, it was described at the time
of opening as 'Glasgow's first
skyscraper hotel' and was erected on
the site of a monumental mason's
yard – for many years an
incongruous feature of Glasgow's
most famous street. Rooftop
kennels were provided where hotel
residents, intent on seeing the
wonders of the Empire Exhibition,
opened on May 3rd, could have
their dogs looked after during their
absence. In October 1938 a cocktail
bar was added to the Beresford's
amenities; designed by the hotel's
managing director, W. Beresford
Inglis, it was situated on the ground
floor, in the front, east corner of the
building, and was presided over by
Canadian-born Mr. J. Macnamara,
late of London's San Marco, Blue
Train and Monseigneur
establishments.

105

Belgrove Hotel, 609 Gallowgate,
June 1937; designed by C.J.
McNair in 1935. Actually a
working-men's hostel, with
characteristic Moderne styling; the
exterior is rendered in horizontal
bands of brick, faïence and cement.

Domestic

Under the influence of Continental Modernism, avant-garde interiors of the early-Thirties had all the elusive charm of operating theatres, with ascetic bare walls (frequently white-distempered), strip-lights and steel furniture. 'It is almost becoming bad form to display any taste for ornament, even for good ornament ...' noted *The Studio Year Book of Decorative Art* for 1934, adding, 'The reaction against superfluous objects and aimless ornament has gone the full length, until anything short of the hygienic standards of a hospital dormitory is looked upon with suspicion.' However, by the late-Thirties, growing antipathy towards starkly plain interiors and monochrome effects had led to renewed interested in warm pastel shades and decorative accessories (including some formerly despised Victorian bibelots), together with a preference for substantial furniture – bulky armchairs and couches, and chunky sideboards and built-in fitments.

Some brave souls, determinedly abreast of the times, overcame the prejudices of local authorities and the opposition of irate neighbours in order to build houses on the lines of Continental 'machines for living in', flat-roofed (in wilful defiance of the North European climate), with verandahs and sun terraces, horizontal metal casement windows and the occasional nautical porthole. Not surprisingly, the great majority of these assymetrical white finished brick or concrete dwellings were built in the pollution-free and comparatively mild South of England. Such trend-setting individuals were in a very small minority in any case; contemporary design – whether Modernist or Moderne – was much more acceptable to the general public when taken in small homeopathic doses in the course of shopping expeditions or visits to the cinema. For the most part the ubiquitous 'bungaloid growths' of the Thirties were singularly uninspired in design, though a little sub Art Deco – a fire surround, perhaps, some leaded glass or a front gate emblazoned with a sunray burst – was certainly not lacking. As likely as not the proud owner of the average suburban bungalow (priced in the region of £550–£650) would have furnished it in the popular 'Tudorbethan' manner, though 'modernistic' dining room and bedroom suites were readily available through hire-purchase firms and department stores. Decorative accessories in the contemporary idiom included geometric-patterned fireside rugs and strength-through-joy ladies, adroitly balancing electric globes. For people with leanings in the direction of aesthetic severity, chromium-plated or enamelled steel furniture was marketed by Thonet, Cox and Co. and Pel Ltd. The long-established firm of Thonet Brothers Ltd. were already well-known for their elegant and sturdy bentwood chairs (still to be seen in some cafés and restaurants) when they began to produce tubular steel chairs to the designs of Le Corbusier, Marcel Breuer and others. When asked his opinion of steel furniture, that great traditionalist Sir Edwin Lutyens wittily replied: 'It is the kind of furniture I would not steal ... I do not see a home with it, there is no place for the cat to hide.'

Service flats were a sign of the times: some members of the middle classes were now living on greatly reduced incomes, while domestic servants were no longer a prolific and docile breed. In the Twenties many villas and terraced houses were split up into smaller dwellings, and the Thirties saw the appearance of purpose-built service flats. In 1938–9 the ambitious development known as Kelvin Court, consisting of two huge Moderne-style blocks, was erected at Anniesland, the culmination of that *drang nach Westen* which, for prosperous Glaswegians, had begun over a century before with the creation of Blythswood 'new town'. Kelvin Court was designed by J.N. Fatkin for Messrs. Alex. Woolf (Builders and Contractors) Ltd., of Newcastle upon Tyne. The blocks were brick-faced, with artificial stone dressings, and contained 100 flats; with war imminent, a bomb-proof shelter was installed in the basement of each block.

106

Sitting-room in service flat, 9 Devonshire Terrace, August 1935. It was in the interwar period that many Victorian mansions in Glasgow's west end were sub-divided for the first time.

Detached house in process of construction, 9 Lawers Road, Mansewood (March 1936). The smooth cement rendering, metal framed windows and flat roof show the influence of Continental Modernism, albeit heavily diluted. The house was designed in 1935 by William A. Gladstone.

═ 108-110 ═

Bungalows, 59 Muirhill Avenue (March 1936), 8 Whitemoss Avenue (August 1937) and 42 Springkell Avenue (June 1938). Typical speculative houses of the Thirties, in which Moderne influence is limited to minor decorative details such as the leaded glass.

≡111/112≡

Terraced houses, 30 Whitemoss Avenue (July 1938) and Yoker Mill Road (September 1938); the octagonal windows, angular door surrounds and smooth rendered finish are indications of speculative developer's Deco. In the late-Thirties Messrs. John Lawrence (Glasgow) Ltd. were offering 'a modern labour-saving home for 15/- per week'.

With its polychrome surfaces and decorative enrichments, James Templeton and Company's famous spool Axminster factory in Glasgow's east end (designed by William Leiper and completed in 1892; now part of the Templeton Business Centre) anticipated the flamboyant Art Deco factories of the interwar years. The latter were mostly built to turn out up-to-date products such as car components and labour-saving domestic appliances and were often advertising mediums in their own right. With their large areas of glass (like famous Hardwick Hall, 'more glass than wall'), glittering faïence decoration and landscaped surroundings, the finest Thirties' factories had little in common with the bleak and grimy industrial buildings of the past. Most of the new factories were situated in the Midlands and South, away from the traditional centres of heavy industry. Messrs. Wallis, Gilbert and Partners were responsible for the magnificent Firestone (1929) and Hoover (1932) factories bordering London's Great West Road, and the same firm designed the handsome India Tyre and Rubber factory (1930) at Inchinnan, now a listed building. Like the Firestone factory (partially demolished in 1980 in a shocking act of Government-condoned vandalism) the India Tyre factory has a highly decorated quasi-Egyptian centrepiece, embellished with brightly coloured ceramic tiles.

As one of the world's greatest centres of heavy engineering, Glasgow derived little benefit from the proliferation of Thirties' light industries, but several Glasgow factories and factory administration blocks exhibited Moderne features such as angular, faïence-faced towers, and Henry Wiggin and Co.'s premises at Thornliebank (1938) were clad in polished black glass after the fashion of the Daily Express buildings in London, Manchester and Glasgow.

* * * *

Nowadays tubular lighting all too readily conjures up associations of institutional buildings and workaday interiors, but in the Thirties, the Neon Age, fluorescent and neon lighting fixtures were frequently productive of original and colourful effects. Fluorescent tubes were used in restaurants and other public interiors in white, yellow, green, orange, pink, mauve and blue, and in combinations of these colours. Neon was virtually a new form of decoration; it was extensively employed by firms such as 'Claudgen' (Claude-General Neon Signs Ltd.) and the Franco-British Electrical Co. Ltd. for purposes of illumination and advertising and was used to great effect on the exteriors of news theatres and cinemas; 'Studios One and Two' in London's Oxford Street (1936) is a striking example of varicoloured neon lighting. The towers and terminal features of many different types of buildings were outlined or otherwise decorated with neon. Huge neon advertisements, attached to railway bridges or the gables of buildings, extolled the merits of popular brands of port and whisky, while the lettering on shop fascias was frequently combined with neon tubing. In this country the further development of neon was arrested by the wartime blackout and post-war austerity, but in the USA, its spiritual home, neon sculpture went on to transform the American skyline, achieving its apotheosis in Las Vegas.

Tollcross YMCA Institute, 1161
Tollcross Road, February 1935;
designed the previous year by John
Easton. The Moderne-detailed
central feature contained the
vestibule, hall and staircase.

114

Entrance to Shawfield greyhound racing stadium, 137 Shawfield Drive, photographed in March 1937. The gates with their tiled gateposts and wrought iron lamps were designed in 1936 by John Easton.

Industrial buildings showing varying degrees of Moderne influence:

═══ 115 ═══

Administration block of the Craigpark Electric Cable Co. Ltd., 242 Flemington Street, Springburn, March 1932 (Messrs. Wylie, Wright and Wylie, architects, 1930).

═══ 116 ═══

Askit laboratories and factory, 89 Saracen Street, Possilpark, February 1933; designed the previous year by William B. White.

═══ 117 ═══

Cyro Works (Farquharson Brothers Ltd., carbon paper manufacturers), 41 Sutcliffe Road, photographed in July 1936.

═══ 118 ═══

Leyland Motors Ltd., offices and service dept., 5 Mauchline Street, September 1938.

═══ 119 ═══

Zenith Works (Henry Wiggin and Co. Ltd.), 775 Boydstone Road, Thornliebank, April 1939. Notice the use of obscured glass bricks, increasingly employed in the late-Thirties for external wall surfaces as well as for partitions, screens and other internal features.

Electricity as a source of illumination was by no means universal in the early-Thirties – it had in fact a novelty value difficult for us to grasp today. Advertisements outlined in neon brought a whiff of Broadway to several well-known Glasgow thoroughfares after dark.

120

Jamaica Bridge, April 1933.

121

Bridge Street, August 1934.

122

Union Street, October 1934.

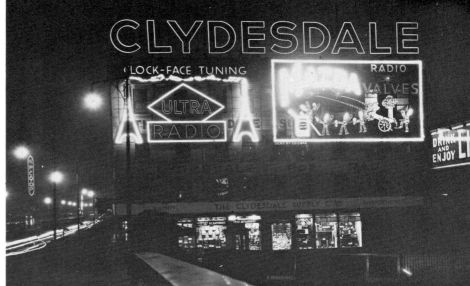

Index

Italicised numbers refer to plates